Contents

KU-498-668

Any words appearing in the text in bold, **like this**,
are explained in the glossary.

What are maps?

A map is a flat drawing of a part of the world. People who make maps are called **cartographers**.

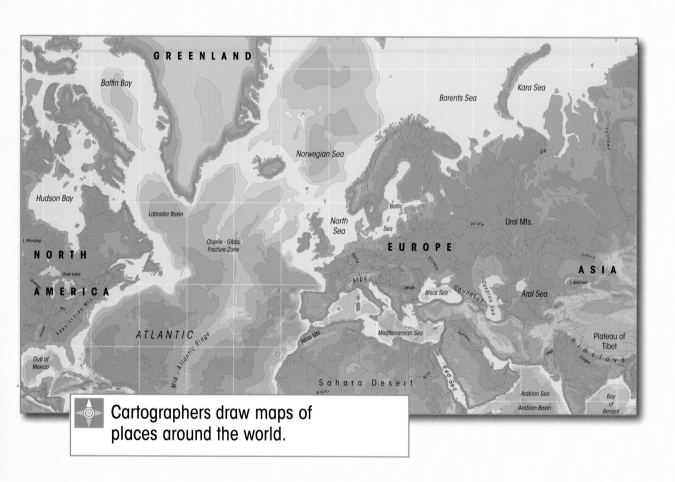

Cartographers draw maps of places around the world.

B51 081 040 0

First Guide to Maps

Mapping the World

**Marta Segal Block and
Daniel R. Block**

WITHDRAWN
FROM THE
ROTHERHAM
PUBLIC
LIBRARY

Heinemann
LIBRARY

www.heinemannlibrary.co.uk
Visit our website to find out more information about Heinemann Library books.

To order:
☎ Phone 44 (0) 1865 888066
▤ Send a fax to 44 (0) 1865 314091
▭ Visit the Heinemann Bookshop at www.heinemannlibrary.co.uk to browse our catalogue and order online.

Heinemann Library is an imprint of Capstone Global Library Limited, a company incorporated in England and Wales having its registered office at 7 Pilgrim Street, London, EC4V 6LB – Registered company number: 6695582

Heinemann is a registered trademark of Pearson Education Limited, under licence to Capstone Global Library Limited

Text © Capstone Global Library Limited 2008
First published in hardback in 2008
Paperback edition first published in 2009

The moral rights of the proprietor have been asserted.

All rights reserved. No part of this publication may be reproduced in any form or by any means (including photocopying or storing it in any medium by electronic means and whether or not transiently or incidentally to some other use of this publication) without the written permission of the copyright owner, except in accordance with the provisions of the Copyright, Designs and Patents Act 1988 or under the terms of a licence issued by the Copyright Licensing Agency, Saffron House, 6–10 Kirby Street, London EC1N 8TS (www.cla.co.uk). Applications for the copyright owner's written permission should be addressed to the publisher.

Editorial: Cassie Mayer and Sian Smith
Design: Jennifer Lacki, Kimberly R. Miracle, and Betsy Wernert
Production: Duncan Gilbert

Illustrated by Mapping specialists
Originated by Modern Age
Printed and bound in China by South China Printing Co. Ltd

ISBN: 978 0 431 12783 5 (hardback)
12 11 10 09 08
10 9 8 7 6 5 4 3 2 1

ISBN: 978 0 431 12788 0 (paperback)
13 12 11 10 09
10 9 8 7 6 5 4 3 2 1

British Library Cataloguing in Publication Data
Block, Marta Segal

Mapping the world. - (First guide to maps)
1. World maps - Juvenile literature 2. Globes - Juvenile literature 3. Maps - Juvenile literature
I. Title II. Block, Daniel, 1967-
912

Acknowledgements
The author and publishers are grateful to the following for permission to reproduce copyright material: ©Corbis pp. **20c** (Arctic, Royalty Free), **27** (zefa/ Jason Horowitz); ©Getty Images pp. **20a b** (rainforest, Royalty Free; desert, Royalty Free); ©Map Resources p. **4**; ©Superstock p. **6** (Royalty Free); ©The Bridgeman Art Library p. **26** (John Carter Brown Library, Brown University, RI, USA).

Cover image reproduced with permission of ©NASA.

Every effort has been made to contact copyright holders of any material reproduced in this book. Any omissions will be rectified in subsequent printings if notice is given to the publishers.

Disclaimer
All the Internet addresses (URLs) given in this book were valid at the time of going to press. However, due to the dynamic nature of the Internet, some addresses may have changed, or sites may have changed or ceased to exist since publication. While the author and publisher regret any inconvenience this may cause readers, no responsibility for any such changes can be accepted by either the author or the publisher.

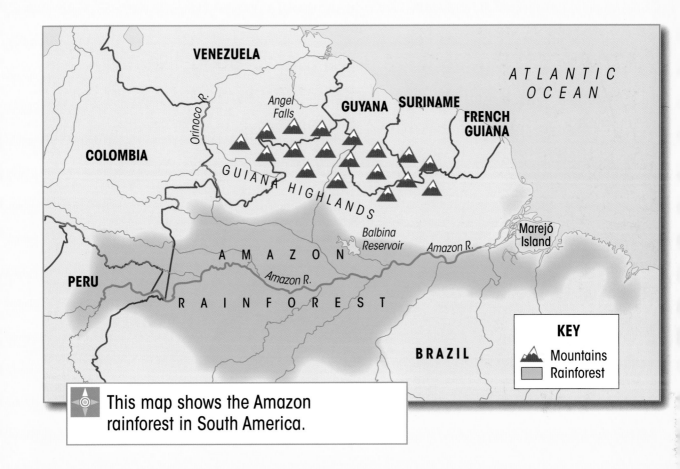

VENEZUELA

ATLANTIC OCEAN

Orinoco R.

Angel Falls

GUYANA   SURINAME

FRENCH GUIANA

COLOMBIA

GUIANA HIGHLANDS

Balbina Reservoir

Amazon R.

Marejó Island

A M A Z O N

Amazon R.

PERU

R A I N F O R E S T

BRAZIL

KEY

⛰ Mountains
▨ Rainforest

This map shows the Amazon rainforest in South America.

Maps teach us about the world. We can use them to find the location of places. We can use them to study physical features such as mountains or lakes. We can also use maps to learn about people who live in different places around the world.

Globes and maps

A **globe** is a model of the Earth that is round, like a ball.
It shows the location of countries and large bodies of water.
A globe is useful for getting a picture of the Earth's features.
But a globe cannot show as much detail as a map.

A globe's size and shape can make it difficult to use.

A map shows the Earth's features on a flat surface. **Cartographers** change the shape and size of things on the Earth. They do this do to fit the round Earth onto a flat map.

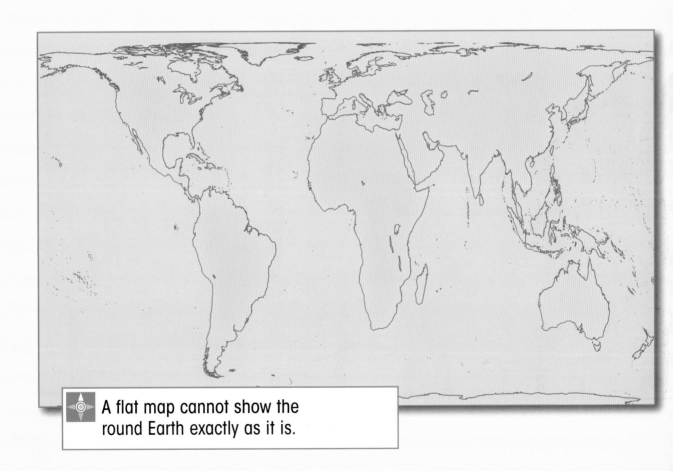

A flat map cannot show the round Earth exactly as it is.

Reading maps

Maps have many features that help you read them. Most maps have a title that tells you what the map is about. Maps also have a **key**. The key tells you what the **symbols** on the map mean. Symbols are small pictures or shapes that stand for things in real life.

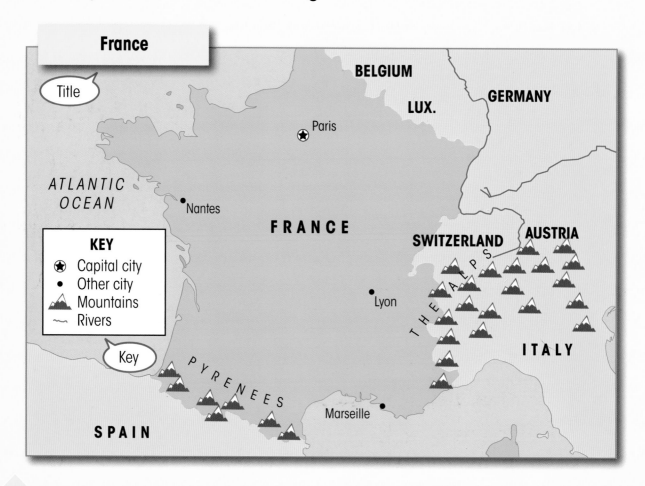

France

Title

BELGIUM

LUX.

GERMANY

Paris

ATLANTIC
OCEAN

Nantes

F R A N C E

SWITZERLAND

AUSTRIA

KEY
★ Capital city
• Other city
⛰ Mountains
〜 Rivers

Lyon

T H E   A L P S

Key

P Y R E N E E S

ITALY

Marseille

S P A I N

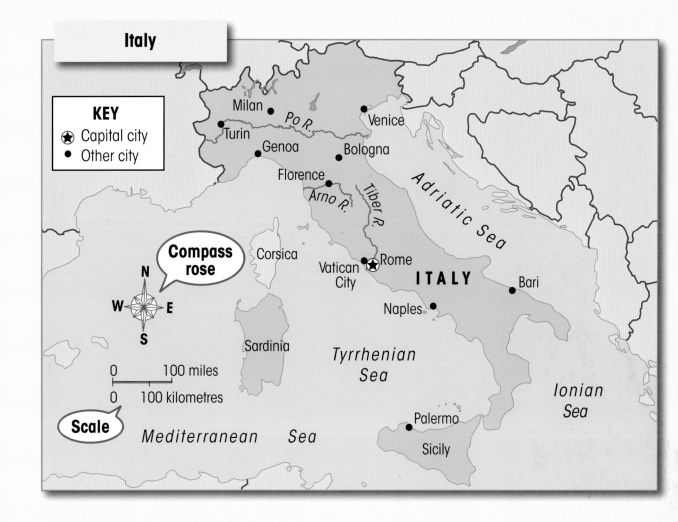

Italy

KEY
⭐ Capital city
● Other city

Milan
Turin
Po R.
Venice
Genoa
Bologna
Florence
Arno R.
Tiber R.
Adriatic Sea

Compass rose

N
W   E
S

Corsica
Vatican City
Rome
ITALY
Bari
Naples

0   100 miles
0   100 kilometres

Scale

Sardinia
Tyrrhenian Sea
Ionian Sea
Mediterranean Sea
Palermo
Sicily

The **compass rose** is a feature that shows direction. The four main directions are north, south, east, and west.

The **scale** is a feature that tells you how far apart things are in real life. It shows how many kilometres or miles equal every centimetre or inch.

Lines around the world

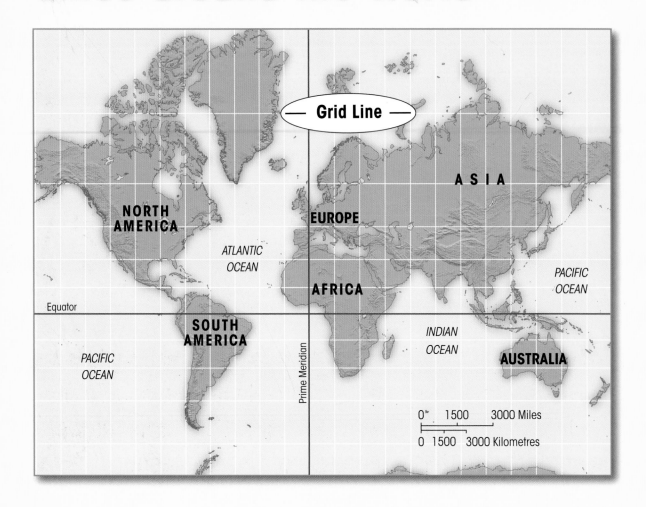

Grid Line

NORTH AMERICA

EUROPE

ASIA

ATLANTIC OCEAN

AFRICA

PACIFIC OCEAN

Equator

SOUTH AMERICA

INDIAN OCEAN

AUSTRALIA

PACIFIC OCEAN

Prime Meridian

0   1500   3000 Miles

0   1500   3000 Kilometres

Many maps have thin lines that look like a net thrown over the map. These are called **grid** lines. They can be used to find the location of places.

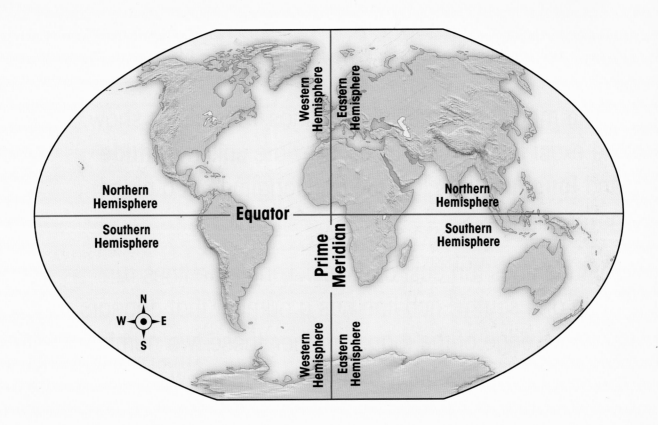

The **Equator** and the **Prime Meridian** are special grid lines. The Equator is halfway between the North Pole and South Pole. It divides the world into two halves, or **hemispheres**. These are the Northern Hemisphere and Southern Hemisphere.

The Prime Meridian goes from the North Pole to the South Pole. The Prime Meridian also divides the world into the Eastern Hemisphere and Western Hemisphere.

Maps about countries

Some maps show the location of countries and their major cities. These maps are called political maps.

Political maps use colour to show different countries. They use lines to show the **borders** between them. Cities are usually shown with dots. Capital cities may be shown with a star. The capital is the place where leaders of a country meet and work.

It is important to use an up-to-date political map. Countries sometimes change their names and borders.

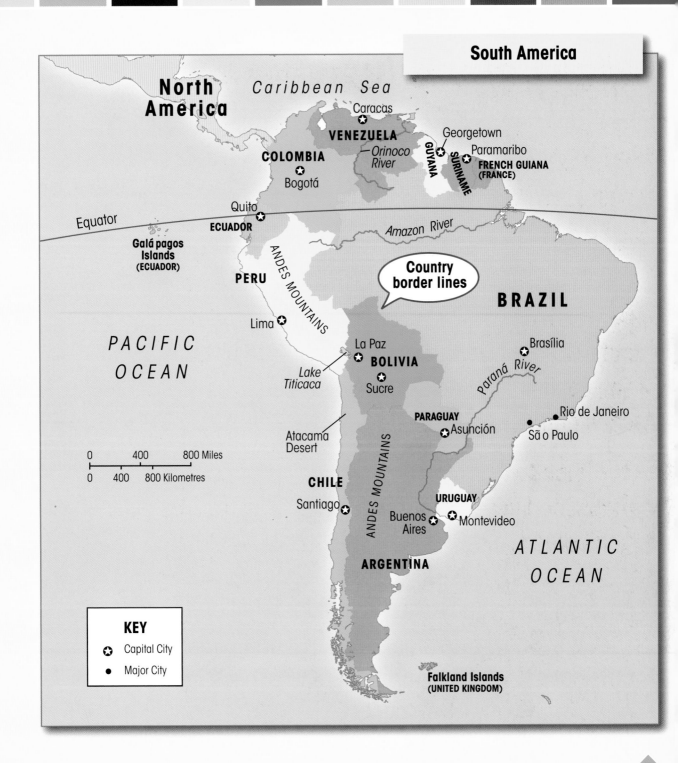

North America

Caribbean Sea

Caracas

VENEZUELA

Georgetown

Paramaribo

COLOMBIA

Orinoco River

GUYANA

SURINAME

FRENCH GUIANA (FRANCE)

Bogotá

Quito

ECUADOR

Equator

Amazon River

Galápagos Islands (ECUADOR)

ANDES MOUNTAINS

Country border lines

BRAZIL

PERU

Brasília

Lima

La Paz

BOLIVIA

Paraná River

PACIFIC OCEAN

Lake Titicaca

Sucre

Rio de Janeiro

São Paulo

PARAGUAY

Asunción

Atacama Desert

ANDES MOUNTAINS

0   400   800 Miles

0   400   800 Kilometres

CHILE

URUGUAY

Santiago

Buenos Aires

Montevideo

ATLANTIC OCEAN

ARGENTINA

KEY

⭐ Capital City

● Major City

Falkland Islands (UNITED KINGDOM)

Maps about land

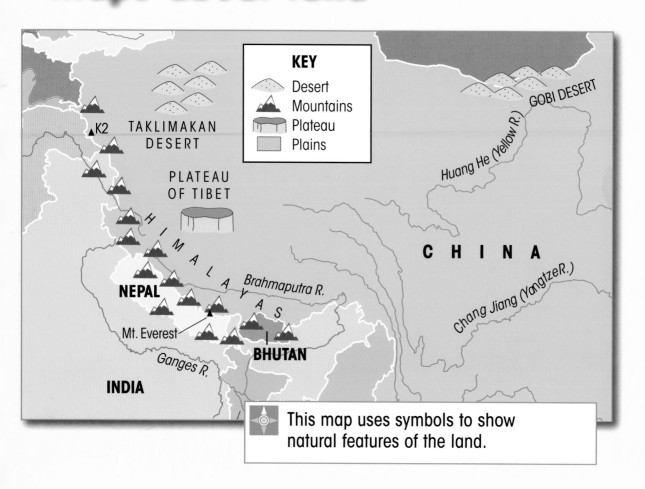

KEY
- Desert
- Mountains
- Plateau
- Plains

K2
TAKLIMAKAN DESERT
PLATEAU OF TIBET
GOBI DESERT
Huang He (Yellow R.)
CHINA
HIMALAYAS
NEPAL
Brahmaputra R.
Chang Jiang (Yangtze R.)
Mt. Everest
BHUTAN
Ganges R.
INDIA

This map uses symbols to show natural features of the land.

Physical maps show the natural features of a place. They can show mountains, deserts, and plains. Some physical maps use **symbols** to show these features.

Some physical maps use different colours to show high and low places. On the map below, brown shows areas where the land is high, such as mountain ranges. Light green shows areas where the land is low.

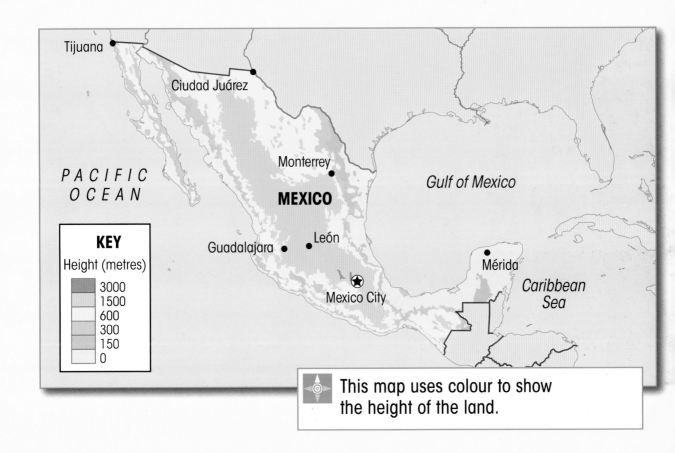

PACIFIC
OCEAN

Tijuana

Ciudad Juárez

Monterrey

MEXICO

Gulf of Mexico

León

Guadalajara

Mérida

Caribbean
Sea

Mexico City

KEY

Height (metres)

3000
1500
600
300
150
0

This map uses colour to show
the height of the land.

Maps about water

Many physical maps show the Earth's bodies of water. You can use them to locate oceans, lakes, and rivers. Water is almost always shown with the colour blue.

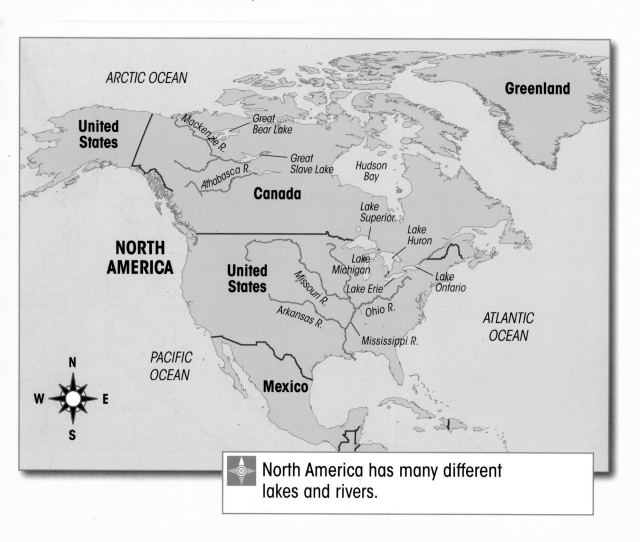

North America has many different lakes and rivers.

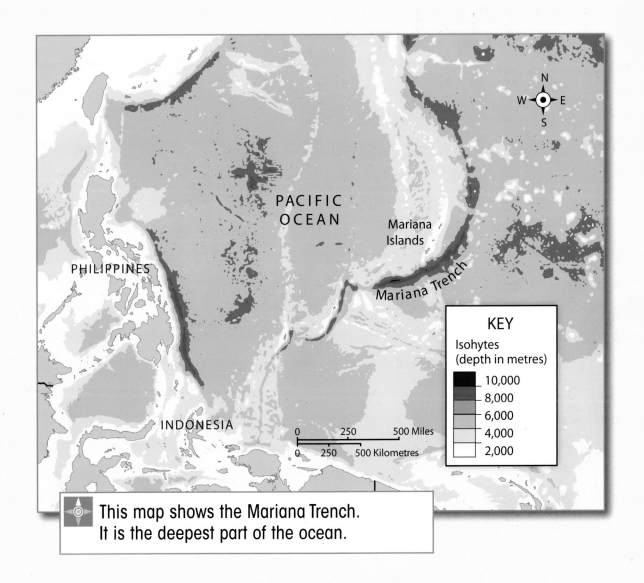

PACIFIC
OCEAN

Mariana
Islands

Mariana Trench

PHILIPPINES

INDONESIA

KEY

Isohytes
(depth in metres)

10,000
8,000
6,000
4,000
2,000

0   250   500 Miles
0 250   500 Kilometres

This map shows the Mariana Trench.
It is the deepest part of the ocean.

Some physical maps show what lies underneath the water.
Some parts of the ocean have mountains and valleys, just
as on land. Maps can also show how deep the water is.

Maps about climate

Climate is the usual weather a place gets over a long period of time. Places in the world have different climates. Some places are hot and dry most of the year. Some places are cold, and some places are wet.

 Can you find these climates on the map on the next page?

Many climate maps use colour to show different climates. It is important to look at the **key** to see what the colours stand for.

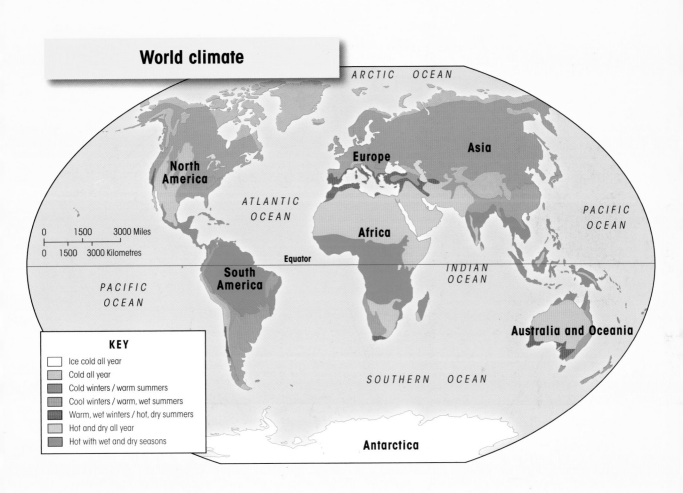

World climate

ARCTIC OCEAN

North America

Europe

Asia

ATLANTIC OCEAN

PACIFIC OCEAN

Africa

| 0 | 1500 | 3000 Miles |
| 0 | 1500 | 3000 Kilometres |

Equator

South America

INDIAN OCEAN

PACIFIC OCEAN

Australia and Oceania

SOUTHERN OCEAN

KEY
- Ice cold all year
- Cold all year
- Cold winters / warm summers
- Cool winters / warm, wet summers
- Warm, wet winters / hot, dry summers
- Hot and dry all year
- Hot with wet and dry seasons

Antarctica

Maps about people

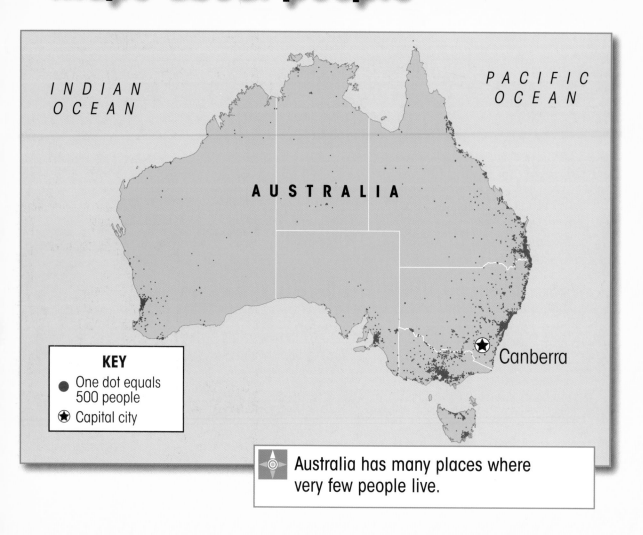

INDIAN OCEAN

PACIFIC OCEAN

AUSTRALIA

KEY
- One dot equals 500 people
- ⊛ Capital city

⊛ Canberra

Australia has many places where very few people live.

Population maps show how many people live in an area. The population map above uses dots to show population.

Some population maps use colour to show how many people live in an area. The map **key** tells you how many people are shown by each colour.

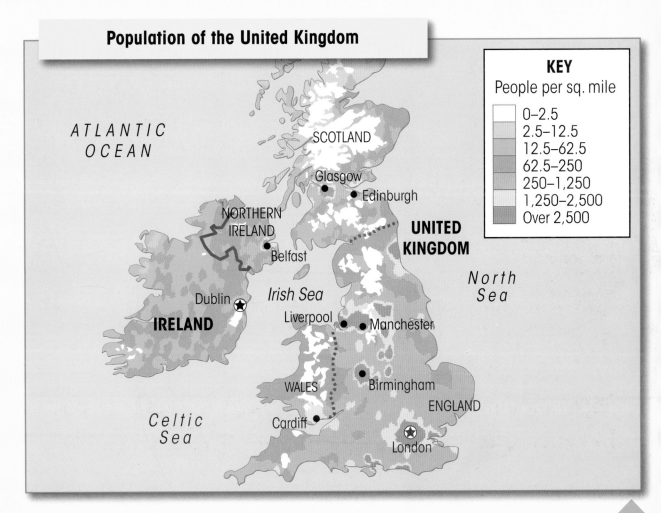

Population of the United Kingdom

KEY
People per sq. mile
0–2.5
2.5–12.5
12.5–62.5
62.5–250
250–1,250
1,250–2,500
Over 2,500

ATLANTIC OCEAN

SCOTLAND

Glasgow
Edinburgh

NORTHERN IRELAND

UNITED KINGDOM

Belfast

North Sea

Dublin
IRELAND

Irish Sea

Liverpool
Manchester

WALES

Birmingham

ENGLAND

Celtic Sea

Cardiff

London

Maps about the economy

A country's **economy** is all the things it makes, sells, and buys. Economic maps can show you what types of jobs people have. They can also show you what foods they grow and what things they make and sell.

Land use in Brazil

VENEZUELA

GUYANA

SURINAME

FRENCH GUIANA

COLOMBIA

ECUADOR

ATLANTIC OCEAN

• Belém

PERU

B R A Z I L

BOLIVIA

⭐ Brasilia

PACIFIC OCEAN

PARAGUAY

• Rio de Janiero

ARGENTINA

KEY

Farming

Livestock raising

Forestry

Trade and manufacturing

⭐ Capital city

• Other cities

This map uses colour to show ways people use the land in the country Brazil.

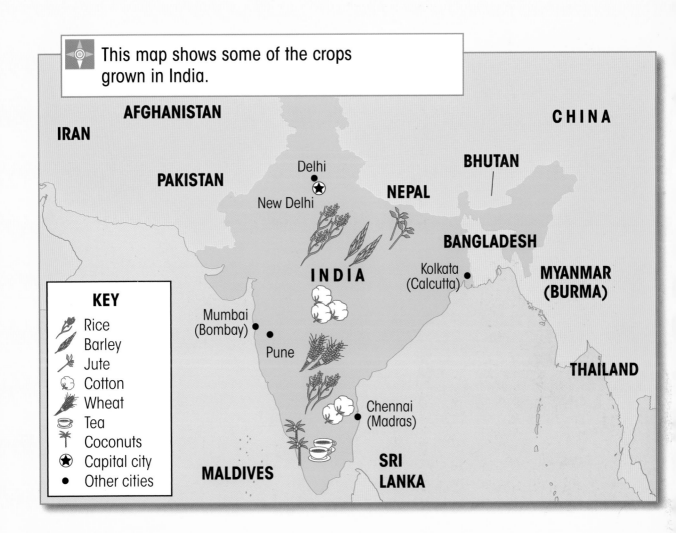

This map shows some of the crops grown in India.

AFGHANISTAN

IRAN

CHINA

PAKISTAN

Delhi
•
New Delhi ⊛

NEPAL

BHUTAN

BANGLADESH

INDIA

Kolkata
(Calcutta) •

MYANMAR
(BURMA)

Mumbai
(Bombay) •
Pune •

THAILAND

Chennai
(Madras) •

KEY

- 🌾 Rice
- 🌿 Barley
- 🌱 Jute
- 🍥 Cotton
- 🌾 Wheat
- 🍵 Tea
- 🌴 Coconuts
- ⊛ Capital city
- • Other cities

MALDIVES

SRI
LANKA

Some maps show you what types of **crops** are grown
in an area. These maps often use **symbols** instead
of colours.

Maps about history

Historical maps tell us what the world used to be like. They also show us what people knew about the world. Some historical maps show the **route** that people took to reach new places.

 This historical map shows the route that the explorer Ferdinand Magellan took on his trip around the world.

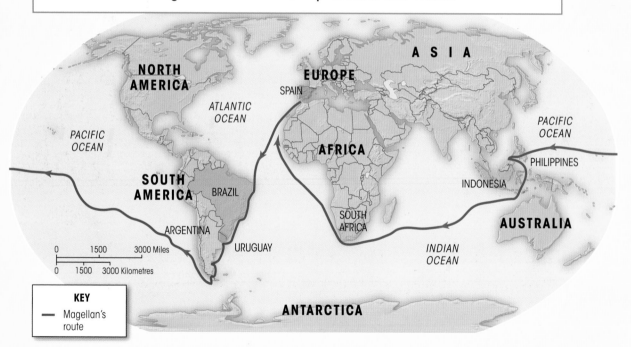

NORTH AMERICA

ATLANTIC OCEAN

PACIFIC OCEAN

SOUTH AMERICA

BRAZIL

ARGENTINA

URUGUAY

EUROPE

SPAIN

AFRICA

SOUTH AFRICA

A S I A

PACIFIC OCEAN

PHILIPPINES

INDONESIA

AUSTRALIA

INDIAN OCEAN

ANTARCTICA

0   1500   3000 Miles
0   1500   3000 Kilometres

KEY
— Magellan's route

With maps, we can learn all kinds of things about the world. The world continues to change, and maps help us to keep up with these changes.

Map activities

The great circle route

For this activity you will need:
- a large world map
- a **globe**
- small pieces of sticky tape
- one or two long pieces of string

1. On a world map, find the United States of America. Now find the state of Illinois. Then find the city of Chicago.

2. Now find Europe on the map. Find the country of Italy. Now find the city of Rome.

3. Tape one end of the string onto Chicago and the other end of the string on Rome. Write down the names of all the cities that your string passes through.

4. Next, do the same thing on a globe. Tape one end of the string to Rome, and one to Chicago. Follow the same path you did on the map along the same line of **latitude**. Make sure you go through the same cities on the globe that you did on the map.

Is this the shortest route between the two cities? Using the globe, find the shortest route. Which route passes the nearest to the North Pole and South Pole?

See if you can find two other cities that are directly east and west of each other and repeat the activity.

Comparing maps

1. Find a **population** map and a physical map of the same country. Check the **scale** to make sure the maps show the same size area.

2. Find the area with the most people. What are the natural features there?

3. Find the area with the fewest people. What are the natural features there? You will probably see that most people live close to rivers, and very few people live in deserts or very cold areas.

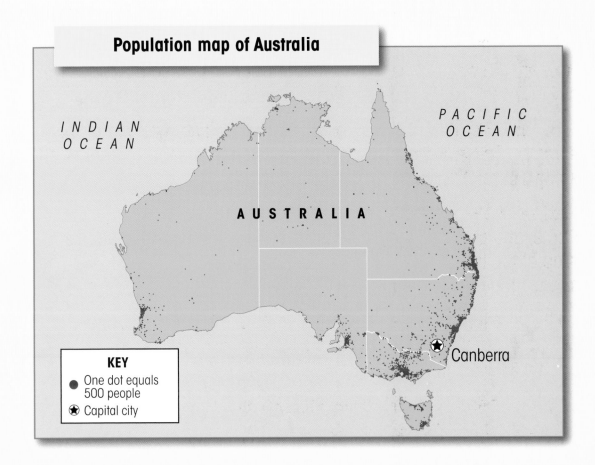

Population map of Australia

INDIAN OCEAN

PACIFIC OCEAN

AUSTRALIA

Canberra

KEY
- One dot equals 500 people
- ⊛ Capital city

Glossary

border imaginary line that divides two places

cartographer person who makes maps

climate usual weather in an area. The weather changes from day to day, but the climate stays the same.

compass rose symbol on a map that shows direction

crop plant that is grown by farmers

economy things a country grows, makes, buys, and sells. It also includes the kinds of jobs people have and how they live.

Equator imaginary line that divides the Earth between north and south

globe round model of the Earth

grid group of lines that are the same distance apart

hemisphere one half of the Earth

key table that shows what the symbols on a map mean

latitude lines on a map or globe that run from east to west

longitude lines on a map or globe that run from north to south

population group or number of people

Prime Meridian imaginary line that divides the Earth between east and west

scale feature on a map that can be used to measure distance

symbol picture that stands for something else

Find out more

Organizations and websites

The websites below may have some advertisements on them. Make sure to ask a trusted adult to look at them with you. You should never give out personal information, including your name and address, without talking to a trusted adult.

Google Maps
Visit Google maps (**maps.google.co.uk**) to find directions from your house to places nearby and far away. Try putting in your address and the address of your school. Do the directions given match your route?

National Geographic
National Geographic provides free maps and photos of the Earth. Visit **www.nationalgeographic.com**.

Books to read

Continents: Europe, Leila Foster and Mary Fox (Heinemann Library, 2006)

Heinemann First Atlas, Daniel Block and Marta Segal Block (Heinemann Library, 2007)

Oxford First Atlas, Patrick Weigand (Oxford University Press, 2005)

World Cultures: Living in the Amazon Rainforest, Anita Ganeri (Raintree, 2007)

Index